"MARKETING MASTERY FOR SMALL BUSINESSES: NAVIGATING STRATEGIES FOR SUCCESS"

I0454588

Contents

Presentation

1.1 Outline of Independent company Showcasing

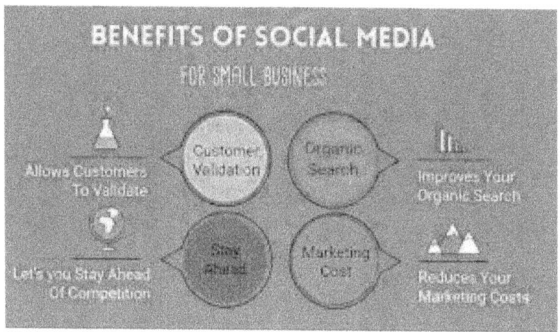

In the powerful scene of business, compelling showcasing assumes a critical part in the outcome of little endeavors. This part gives an exhaustive outline of the central ideas and techniques that structure the groundwork of independent venture showcasing.

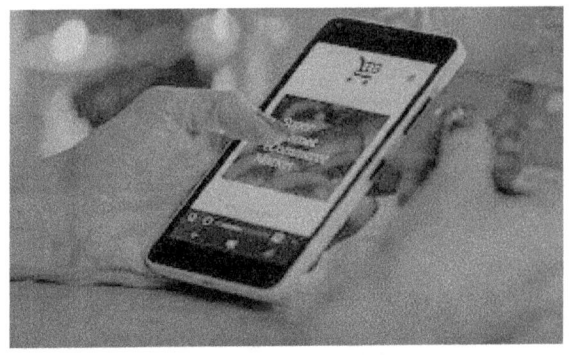

Significance of Successful Advertising Procedures

Figuring out the basic significance of advertising in driving business development. Investigate how key showcasing goes past publicizing to make an enduring effect on brand perceivability, client commitment, and by and large market situating.

As we dive into the complexities of private company promoting, the objective is to furnish you with bits of knowledge and commonsense ways to deal with explore the cutthroat field, interface with your interest group, and fabricate a reasonable presence on the lookout. We should leave on an excursion to open the privileged insights of fruitful independent venture showcasing.

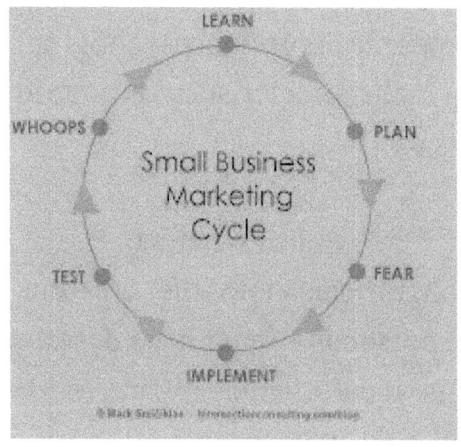

Getting a handle on Your Group

2.1 Distinctive Your Goal Market

Preceding leaving on any publicizing attempts, it's basic to perceive and fathom your goal market. This fragment guides you through the technique associated with describing the specific portion, psychographic, and social characteristics of your ideal clients.

Client Persona Improvement

Hop significant into the creation of client personas - imaginary depictions of your ideal clients. Figure out how to make definite personas that mirror your crowd's different necessities, inclinations, and trouble spots by social affair information, directing statistical surveying, and using bits of knowledge.

You will be in a superior situation to tailor your showcasing messages, items, and administrations to measure up to your clients' assumptions on the off chance that you focus on your objective market and fathom the specifics of their lives. The outing to productive confidential endeavor advancing beginnings with a critical cognizance of people you hope to serve.

Making Your Novel Offer (UVP)

3.1 Characterizing Your Business' Exceptional Selling Focuses

In a packed commercial center, having a Novel Offer (UVP) is urgent for separating your business from rivals. This segment digs into the most common way of distinguishing and articulating the special elements and advantages that make your items or administrations stick out.

Conveying Your UVP Actually

Creating a convincing UVP is just a portion of the fight; Equally important is how you convey it to your intended audience. Investigate methodologies for passing your UVP on through different promoting channels, guaranteeing that your informing reverberates with the particular requirements and wants of your crowd.

You can build a solid foundation for attracting and retaining customers by focusing on what sets your company apart and clearly articulating it. This segment guides you through the moves toward make an UVP that separates your business as well as spellbinds the hearts and brains of your likely clients.

Building a Web-based Presence

4.1 Site Advancement and Improvement

In the computerized age, a strong web-based presence is crucial for private companies. This part directs you through the most common way of making and enhancing your site to act as a strong center for your web-based exercises.

4.1.1 Creating an Engaging Website

Investigate the essential components of a website that is both user-friendly and visually appealing. From instinctive route to convincing substance, find the parts that add to a positive client experience.

4.1.2 Website streamlining (Web optimization)

Comprehend the basics of Web optimization to upgrade your site's perceivability on web search tools. Figure out how to lead catchphrase research, upgrade on-page components, and assemble quality backlinks for further developed search rankings.

4.2 Virtual Entertainment Systems for Independent companies

Virtual entertainment stages offer extraordinary open doors for private ventures to associate with their crowd. This part investigates viable systems for utilizing virtual entertainment to assemble brand mindfulness, draw in clients, and direct people to your site.

4.2.1 Picking the Right Virtual Entertainment Stages

Figure out which virtual entertainment stages line up with your interest group and business objectives. Investigate the special elements of every stage and how they can be bridled to augment your internet-based presence.

4.2.2 Substance Creation and Commitment

Dive into the specialty of making convincing substance for web-based entertainment. Know how to tailor your messages to appeal to your target audience, encourage interaction, and cultivate a sense of brand community.

By decisively creating and enhancing your web-based presence, you position your private company for outcome in the advanced scene. Whether through a very much created site or drawing in web-based entertainment systems, this part outfits you with the devices to explore and flourish in the internet-based domain.

Content Showcasing for Independent companies

5.1 Making Convincing Substance

Content promoting is a foundation of building brand authority and drawing in with your crowd. This part investigates the workmanship and study of making content that reverberates with your objective market.

5.1.1 Substance Arranging and System

Foster an exhaustive substance technique that lines up with your business objectives. Learn how to choose topics for your content, make a content calendar, and write a story that all fits together and helps your brand stand out.

5.1.2 Fitting Substance to Your Crowd

Grasp the significance of crowd division in happy creation. Investigate methods for fitting your substance to address the particular requirements, interests, and problem areas of various fragments inside your interest group.

5.2 Writing for a blog and Content Circulation

Writing for a blog is an amazing asset for laying out thought initiative and driving natural traffic to your site. This segment dives into the subtleties of viable writing for a blog and methodologies for dispersing your substance across different channels.

5.2.1 Making Drawing in Blog Entries

Investigate the components of an effective blog entry, from eye catching titles to convincing narrating. Figure out how to enhance your blog content for web indexes and support social sharing.

5.2.2 Utilizing Content Conveyance Channels

Find the assorted channels accessible for appropriating your substance, including virtual entertainment, email advertising, and outsider stages. Create a multi-channel dispersion methodology to boost the range and effect of your substance.

By excelling at content showcasing, you improve your image's perceivability as well as lay out a significant association with your crowd. You can use the insights in this section to create and distribute content that captivates, educates, and converts.

Utilizing Email Promoting 6.1 Structure an Email Rundown Email showcasing is as yet a useful asset for building associations with clients and expanding deals. This part guides you through the technique engaged with building and managing a fruitful email list.

6.1.1 Making Overwhelming

Lead Magnets Investigate ways of utilizing important lead magnets to get your crowd to pursue your email list. From computerized books to choose offers, sort out some way to give inspirations that resound your ideal vested party.

6.1.2 Completing Pick In Procedures

Grasp the different select in procedures to foster your email list normally. Find techniques that compare to the inclinations and activities of your crowd, like spring up advertisements on sites and advancements via virtual entertainment.

6.2 Powerful Email Lobbies for Independent ventures An essential methodology is expected to make successful email crusades. This part dives into the basic parts of arranging and executing compelling email campaigns.

6.2.1 Division and Personalization

Explore the benefits of isolating your email list considering portion, lead, or responsibility principles. Learn how to make your emails' content more relevant and engaging by tailoring it to various audiences.

6.2.2 Robotization and Stream Missions

Track down the power of email robotization in passing on assigned and optimal messages. Execute stream missions to support leads, locally accessible new clients, and reconnect latent allies.

By harnessing the capacity of email advancing, you can make modified and huge relationship with your group. This section outfits you with the gadgets to create a responsive email overview and setup campaigns that drive responsibility and changes for your confidential endeavor.

Neighborhood Promoting Systems

7.1 Utilizing Neighborhood Website design enhancement

Neighborhood site design improvement (Web optimization) is fundamental for private ventures hoping to interface with their local area. This part investigates the procedures to improve your neighborhood online perceivability and draw in clients in your geological region.

7.1.1 Google My Business Advancement

Gain proficiency with the significance of enhancing your Google My Business profile. Investigate moves toward guarantee precise business data, accumulate client audits, and increment your perceivability in neighborhood list items.

7.1.2 Neighborhood Watchword Exploration

Comprehend the subtleties of neighborhood watchword examination to tailor your substance and site for area explicit inquiries. Find devices and methods to recognize the watchwords that make the biggest difference to your neighborhood crowd.

7.2 Local area Commitment and Associations

Building areas of strength for an inside your nearby local area goes past internet based techniques. This section examines practical offline strategies for connecting with your community and forming meaningful partnerships.

7.2.1 Partaking in Neighborhood Occasions

Investigate the advantages of partaking in neighborhood occasions and sponsorships. Figure out how to pick occasions that line up with your image and influence them to expand mindfulness and cultivate local area associations.

7.2.2 Teaming up with Nearby Organizations

Find the force of organizations with other nearby organizations. Investigate systems for making commonly helpful coordinated efforts that can extend your scope and offer added benefit to your clients.

By joining nearby Search engine optimization strategies with disconnected local area commitment, you can make a comprehensive neighborhood promoting technique that reinforces your binds with the local area and positions your private venture as a confided in nearby asset. This part gives noteworthy experiences to help you explore and prevail in the nearby market.

Disconnected Showcasing Strategies

8.1 Print Promoting and Guarantee

Print promoting stays a substantial and significant method for contacting your crowd. This segment investigates the different types of print media and insurance that can supplement your private company promoting endeavors.

8.1.1 Planning Successful Print Materials

Find the vital standards of planning convincing print materials, including business cards, pamphlets, and flyers. Figure out how to make outwardly engaging materials that impart your image message really.

8.1.2 Setting Print Advertisements Decisively

Investigate systems for putting print ads in neighborhood distributions, papers, and local area sheets. Comprehend the significance of focusing on your crowd and picking the right print channels for greatest effect.

Up close and personal cooperations are significant for building connections and creating business leads. This segment digs into systems administration methodologies and occasion investment to extend your independent venture reach.

8.2.1 Compelling Systems administration Strategies

Figure out how to explore organizing occasions, both on the web and disconnected, to associate with likely clients and industry peers. Comprehend the specialty of creating a convincing short presentation and building significant associations.

8.2.2 Facilitating and Taking part in Occasions

Investigate the advantages of facilitating or taking part in occasions pertinent to your industry or local area. From studios to expos, comprehend how occasions can upgrade brand perceivability and lay out your business as an expert in your field.

By consolidating disconnected promoting strategies, you can make a balanced showcasing procedure that stretches out past the computerized domain. This segment gives experiences into utilizing print media actually and taking full advantage of

eye to eye cooperation's to fortify
your independent company presence.

Checking and Dissecting Showcasing Execution

9.1 Key Measurements for Independent ventures

Following and dissecting key measurements is crucial for check the outcome of your promoting endeavors. This part frames the vital exhibition pointers that private companies ought to screen to survey their promoting influence.

9.1.1 Site Investigation

Investigate the experiences given by site examination apparatuses. Figure out how to decipher measurements, for example, traffic, skip rate, and transformation rates to grasp client conduct and streamline your web-based presence.

9.1.2 Online Entertainment Measurements

Plunge into the universe of web-based entertainment examination. Comprehend how to quantify commitment, reach, and change on different stages, permitting you to refine your web-based entertainment procedures in light of information driven experiences.

Using Analytics Data is only useful when it is used to help make decisions. This part directs you through the method involved with deciphering advertising examination and making vital acclimations to streamline your private venture promoting endeavors.

9.2.1 A/B Testing and Iterative Improvement

Investigate the idea of A/B testing to explore different avenues regarding various components of your promoting efforts. Figure out how to utilize iterative improvement in view of information examination to upgrade your systems persistently.

9.2.2 Adjusting to Market Changes

Comprehend the significance of remaining deft despite market changes. Investigate procedures for adjusting your showcasing approach in light of developing shopper ways of behaving, industry patterns, and serious scenes.

By becoming amazing at observing and breaking down promoting execution, you enable your independent company to pursue informed choices, refine techniques, and expand the effect of your showcasing endeavors. You can use the insights in this section to effectively navigate the marketing analytics world.

Planning for Independent venture Promoting

10.1 Apportioning Assets Actually

Key assignment of assets is vital for independent ventures expecting to take full advantage of their promoting financial plan. For best results, this section will walk you through budgeting and resource allocation.

10.1.1 Putting forth Practical Showcasing Objectives

Lay out clear and quantifiable promoting objectives that line up with your general business goals. Figure out how to set sensible focuses on that guide your planning choices and give a system to surveying achievement.

10.1.2 Deciding Advertising Channels and Strategies

Investigate different advertising channels and strategies, both on the web and disconnected. Figure out the expense ramifications of each and focus on those that reverberate most with your interest group, guaranteeing a successful distribution of assets.

Compelling showcasing doesn't necessarily in all cases require a significant spending plan. This segment gives innovative and minimal expense showcasing thoughts custom-made for independent ventures hoping to augment their effect without burning through every last cent.

10.2.1 Utilizing Virtual Entertainment Natural Reach

Investigate methodologies for augmenting your virtual entertainment presence without huge promotion spend. From connecting with content to local area building, find ways of utilizing natural reach to its fullest potential.

10.2.2 Cooperative Advertising Drives

Gain proficiency with the force of cooperation with different organizations and powerhouses. Find minimal expense organization valuable open doors that can extend your span, improve believability, and create shared benefits.

By drawing closer planning with an essential mentality and investigating practical promoting thoughts, independent ventures can accomplish critical outcomes inside their monetary requirements. This part gives experiences to assist you with settling on informed choices and get the most worth from your advertising financial plan.